COZY FASHION ACCENTS

Chevrons, cables, and other striking stitch patterns bring fabulous style to these knit boot cuffs, ear warmers, and scarves. Choose from 10 sets to make warm fashions for yourself or your family and friends.

D1609327

LEISURE ARTS, INC. • Maumelle, Arkansas

CHEVRON SEED STITCH SET

 EASY

SHOPPING LIST

Yarn (Medium Weight) 4

[3.5 ounces, 170 yards
(100 grams, 156 meters) per skein]:

☐ 3 skeins

Knitting Needle

16" (40.5 cm) Circular,

☐ Size 9 (5.5 mm)

or size needed for gauge

Additional Supplies

☐ Marker

GAUGE INFORMATION

In Body pattern,

16 sts = 4½" (11.5 cm);

22 rnds/rows = 4" (10 cm)

INSTRUCTIONS

Boot Cuff (Make 2)

Finished Size:

5½" long x 13½" upper
circumference (14 cm x 34.5 cm)

RIBBING

Cast on 48 sts, place marker to
mark beginning of rnd *(see Circular
Knitting and Markers, page 29)*.

Rnds 1-11: (K2, P2) around.

BODY

Rnd 1 (Right side)**:** (P1, K3) around.

Rnd 2: ★ K1, P1, K5, P1; repeat from ★
around.

Rnd 3: K2, P1, (K3, P1) around to last
st, K1.

Rnd 4: K3, P1, K1, P1, ★ K5, P1, K1, P1;
repeat from ★ around to last 2 sts, K2.

Rnds 5-20: Repeat Rnds 1-4, 4 times.

Bind off all sts in **knit**.

Ear Warmer

Finished Size: 3¾" wide x 18"
circumference (9.5 cm x 45.5 cm)

Cast on 64 sts, place marker to mark
beginning of rnd.

Rnd 1 (Right side)**:** (P1, K3) around.

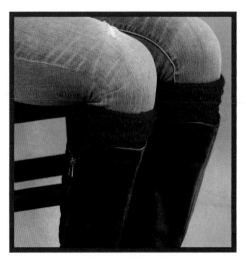

● ● ● ● ● ●

Rnd 2: ★ K1, P1, K5, P1; repeat from ★ around.

Rnd 3: K2, P1, (K3, P1) around to last st, K1.

Rnd 4: K3, P1, K1, P1, ★ K5, P1, K1, P1; repeat from ★ around to last 2 sts, K2.

Rnds 5-20: Repeat Rnds 1-4, 4 times.

Bind off all sts in **purl**.

Instructions continued on page 9.

LITTLE SHELLS SET

● ● ● ● ● ● ● ● ● ● ● ● ● ● ● ● ●

◼◼☐☐ **EASY +**

SHOPPING LIST

Yarn (Medium Weight)
[7 ounces, 364 yards
(198 grams, 333 meters) per skein]:
☐ 2 skeins

Knitting Needle
16" (40.5 cm) Circular,
☐ Size 9 (5.5 mm)
   or size needed for gauge

Additional Supplies
☐ Marker

GAUGE INFORMATION
In Body pattern,
2 repeats (14 sts) and
22 rnds/rows = 4" (10 cm)

TECHNIQUES USED
📹 Knit increase **(Figs. 3a & b,**
    page 30)
📹 YO **(Figs. 5a & b, page 30)**
📹 P3 tog **(Fig. 8, page 31)**

INSTRUCTIONS
Boot Cuff (Make 2)
Finished Size:
   5½" long x 14" upper circumference
   (14 cm x 35.5 cm)

RIBBING
Cast on 48 sts, 📹 place marker to
mark beginning of rnd *(see Circular
Knitting and Markers, page 29).*

Rnds 1-11: (K2, P2) around.

BODY
Rnd 1 (Right side): Work knit increase,
knit around: 49 sts.

Rnd 2: Knit around.

Rnd 3: ★ YO, P1, P3 tog, P1, YO, K2;
repeat from ★ around.

Rnds 4-6: Knit around.

Rnds 7-18: Repeat Rnds 3-6, 3 times.

Bind off all sts in **knit**.

Ear Warmer

Finished Size: 3¾" wide x 20" circumference (9.5 cm x 51 cm)

Cast on 70 sts, place marker to mark beginning of rnd.

Rnd 1 (Right side)**:** Purl around.

Rnds 2-4: Knit around.

Rnd 5: ★ YO, P1, P3 tog, P1, YO, K2; repeat from ★ around.

Rnds 6-20: Repeat Rnds 2-5, 3 times; then repeat Rnds 2-4 once **more**.

Bind off all sts in **purl**.

Instructions continued on page 9.

ARCHING CABLES SET

EASY +

SHOPPING LIST

Yarn (Medium Weight)
[3.5 ounces, 170 yards
(100 grams, 156 meters) per skein]:
☐ 3 skeins

Knitting Needle
16" (40.5 cm) Circular,
☐ Size 8 (5 mm)
   or size needed for gauge

Additional Supplies
☐ Marker
☐ Cable needle

GAUGE INFORMATION
In pattern,
   24 sts = 5" (12.75 cm);
   24 rnds/rows = 4" (10 cm)

STITCH GUIDE

🎥 **CABLE 4 BACK**
   (abbreviated C4B) (uses 4 sts)
Slip next 2 sts onto cable needle and
hold in **back** of work, K2 from left
point, K2 from cable needle.

🎥 **CABLE 4 FRONT**
   (abbreviated C4F) (uses 4 sts)
Slip next 2 sts onto cable needle and
hold in **front** of work, K2 from left
point, K2 from cable needle.

TECHNIQUES USED
🎥 Knit increase *(Figs. 3a & b, page 30)*
🎥 K2 tog *(Fig. 6, page 31)*
🎥 P2 tog *(Fig. 7, page 31)*

INSTRUCTIONS
Boot Cuff (Make 2)
Finished Size:
   5½" long x 10" upper
   circumference (14 cm x 25.5 cm)

Cast on 41 sts, 🎥 place marker to
mark beginning of rnd *(see Circular
Knitting and Markers, page 29)*.

Rnd 1 (Right side)**:** K1, (P1, K1)
around.

Rnd 2: P1, (K1, P1) around.

• • • • • •

Rnds 3-16: Repeat Rnds 1 and 2, 7 times.

Rnd 17: (K5, work knit increase) 6 times, K4, work knit increase: 48 sts.

Rnds 18-20: Knit around.

Rnd 21: ★ C4B, K4, C4F; repeat from ★ around.

Rnds 22-24: Knit around.

Rnd 25: ★ C4F, C4B K4; repeat from ★ around.

Rnds 26-28: Knit around.

Rnd 29: ★ C4B, K4, C4F; repeat from ★ around.

Rnds 30 and 31: Knit around.

Rnd 32: ★ (K1, P1) 3 times, K2 tog, (P1, K1) 3 times, P2 tog; repeat from ★ 2 times **more**: 42 sts.

Rnd 33: (P1, K1) around.

Bind off all sts in **purl**.

Ear Warmer

Finished Size: 3½" wide x 15" circumference (9 cm x 38 cm)

Cast on 72 sts, place marker to mark beginning of rnd.

Rnd 1: (K1, P1) around.

Rnd 2 (Right side)**:** (P1, K1) around.

Rnd 3: (K1, P1) around.

Rnds 4-7: Knit around.

Rnd 8: ★ C4B, K4, C4F; repeat from ★ around.

Rnds 9-11: Knit around.

Rnd 12: ★ C4F, C4B, K4; repeat from ★ around.

Rnds 13-15: Knit around.

Rnd 16: ★ C4B, K4, C4F; repeat from ★ around.

Rnds 17 and 18: Knit around.

Rnd 19: (K1, P1) around.

Rnd 20: (P1, K1) around.

Bind off all sts in **purl**.

Scarf

Finished Size: 7" wide x 57" long (18 cm x 145 cm)

Cast on 34 sts.

Row 1: (K1, P1) across.

Row 2 (Right side)**:** (P1, K1) across.

Rows 3-6: Repeat Rows 1 and 2 twice.

Row 7: K1, (P1, K1) twice, P 25, (K1, P1) twice.

Row 8: P1, (K1, P1) twice, K 25, (P1, K1) twice.

Row 9: K1, (P1, K1) twice, P 25, (K1, P1) twice.

Row 10: P1, (K1, P1) twice, ★ C4B, K4, C4F; repeat from ★ once **more**, K1, (P1, K1) twice.

Rows 11-13: Repeat Rows 7-9.

Row 14: P1, (K1, P1) twice, C4F, C4B, K4, C4F, C4B, K5, (P1, K1) twice.

Repeat Rows 7-14 for pattern until piece measures approximately 56" (142 cm) from cast on edge, ending by working Row 9 or Row 13.

Next Row: (P1, K1) across.

Next Row: (K1, P1) across.

Next 4 Rows: Repeat last 2 rows twice.

Bind off all sts in **purl**.

CHEVRON SEED STITCH SET continued from page 3.

Scarf

Finished Size: 9" wide x 59" long
(23 cm x 150 cm)

Cast on 32 sts.

Row 1 (Right side)**:** Slip 1 as if to **knit**, P1, (K1, P1) across.

Row 2: Slip 1 as if to **knit**, K1, (P1, K1) across.

Rows 3-6: Repeat Rows 1 and 2 twice.

Row 7: Slip 1 as if to **knit**, P1, K1, P2, (K3, P1) 5 times, K4, P1, K1, P1.

Row 8: Slip 1 as if to **knit**, K1, P1, K2, P5, K1, (P1, K1, P5, K1) twice, P2, K1, P1, K1.

Row 9: Slip 1 as if to **knit**, P1, K1, P1, K2, P1, (K3, P1) 5 times, K2, P1, K1, P1.

Row 10: Slip 1 as if to **knit**, K1, P1, K1, P2, K1, P1, K1, (P5, K1, P1, K1) twice, P4, K1, P1, K1.

Repeat Rows 7-10 for pattern until piece measures approximately 58" (147.5 cm) from cast on edge, ending by working Row 10.

Last 6 Rows: Repeat Rows 1-6.

Bind off all sts in pattern.

LITTLE SHELLS SET continued from page 5.

Scarf

Finished Size: 10¼" wide x 59" long
(26 cm x 150 cm)

Cast on 36 sts.

Rows 1-5: Slip 1 as if to **knit**, knit across.

Row 6: Slip 1 as if to **knit**, K2, P 30, K3.

Row 7 (Right side)**:** Slip 1 as if to **knit**, K4, ★ YO, P1, P3 tog, P1, YO, K2; repeat from ★ 3 times **more**, K3.

Row 8: Slip 1 as if to **knit**, K2, P 30, K3.

Row 9: Slip 1 as if to **knit**, knit across.

Repeat Rows 6-9 for pattern until piece measures approximately 58" (147.5 cm) from cast on edge, ending by working Row 8.

Last 5 Rows: Slip 1 as if to **knit**, knit across.

Bind off all sts in **knit**.

9

DOUBLE SEED STITCH SET

 **EASY**

SHOPPING LIST

Yarn (Medium Weight)
[3.5 ounces, 170 yards
(100 grams, 156 meters) per skein]:
☐ 3 skeins

Knitting Needle
16" (40.5 cm) Circular,
☐ Size 8 (5 mm)
   or size needed for gauge

Additional Supplies
☐ Marker

GAUGE INFORMATION

In Body pattern,
   16 sts and 24 rnds/rows = 4"
   (10 cm)

INSTRUCTIONS
Boot Cuff (Make 2)
Finished Size:
   5" long x 13" upper circumference
   (12.75 cm x 33 cm)

RIBBING
Cast on 52 sts, 🎥 place marker to
mark beginning of rnd *(see Circular
Knitting and Markers, page 29).*

Rnds 1-13: (K2, P2) around.

BODY

Rnds 1 and 2: (K1, P1) around.

Rnds 3 and 4: (P1, K1) around.

Rnds 5-17: Repeat Rnds 1-4, 3 times;
then repeat Rnd 1 once **more**.

Bind off all sts in **knit**.

• • • • • •

Ear Warmer

Finished Size: 3¾" wide x 18" circumference (9.5 cm x 45.5 cm)

Cast on 72 sts, place marker to mark beginning of rnd.

Rnd 1: Knit around.

Rnd 2: Purl around.

Rnds 3 and 4: (K1, P1) around.

Rnds 5 and 6: (P1, K1) around.

Rnds 7-21: Repeat Rnds 3-6, 3 times; then repeat Rnds 3-5 once **more**.

Rnd 22: Purl around.

Bind off all sts in **purl**.

Instructions continued on page 17.

GARTER STRIPES SET

EASY

SHOPPING LIST

Yarn (Medium Weight) **4**
[7 ounces, 364 yards
(198 grams, 333 meters) per skein]:
☐ 2 skeins

Knitting Needle
16" (40.5 cm) Circular,
☐ Size 8 (5 mm)
or size needed for gauge

Additional Supplies
☐ Marker

GAUGE INFORMATION

In pattern,
16 sts and 24 rnds/rows = 4"
(10 cm)

INSTRUCTIONS
Boot Cuff (Make 2)

Finished Size:

5½" long x 11½" upper
circumference (14 cm x 29 cm)

Cast on 46 sts, place marker to
mark beginning of rnd *(see Circular
Knitting and Markers, page 29)*.

Rnd 1 (Right side)**:** Knit around.

Rnd 2: Purl around.

Rnds 3-20: Repeat Rnds 1 and 2,
9 times.

Rnds 21-34: Knit around.

Rnd 35: Purl around.

Rnd 36: Knit around.

Rnds 37 and 38: Repeat Rnds 35 and
36.

Bind off all sts in **purl**.

● ● ● ● ● ●

Ear Warmer

Finished Size: 4" wide x 17" circumference (10 cm x 43 cm)

Cast on 68 sts, place marker to mark beginning of rnd.

Rnd 1 (Right side)**:** Knit around.

Rnd 2: Purl around.

Rnds 3-6: Repeat Rnds 1 and 2.

Rnds 7-20: Knit around.

Rnd 21: Purl around.

Rnd 22: Knit around.

Rnds 23-26: Repeat Rnds 21 and 22 twice.

Bind off all sts in **purl**.

Instructions continued on page 17.

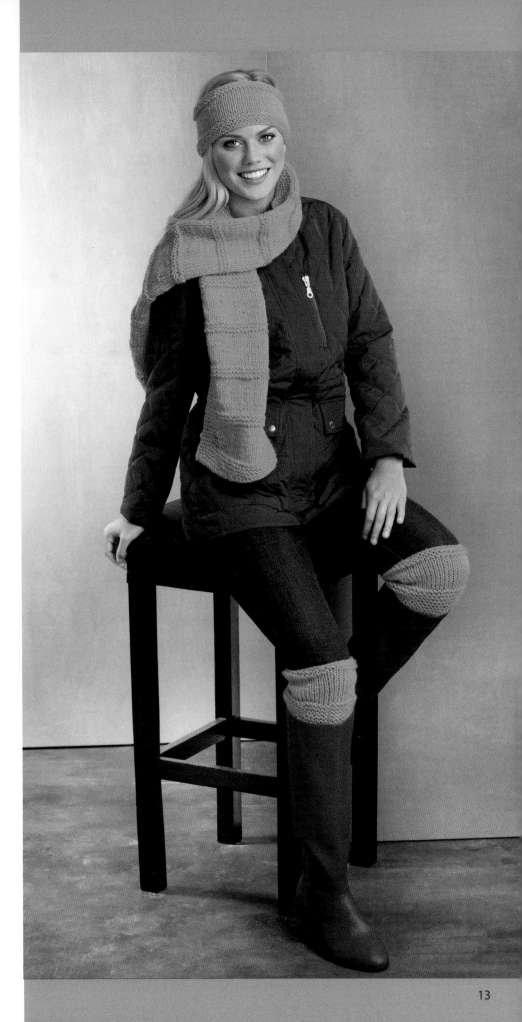

SLIP STITCH SET

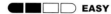
SHOPPING LIST

Yarn (Medium Weight) 🧶**4**

[3.5 ounces, 170 yards
(100 grams, 156 meters) per skein]:
☐ Cream - 3 skeins

[2.5 ounces, 121 yards
(70 grams, 111 meters) per skein]:
☐ Variegated - 2 skeins

Knitting Needle

16" (40.5 cm) Circular,
☐ Size 9 (5.5 mm)
  or size needed for gauge

Additional Supplies

☐ Marker

GAUGE INFORMATION

In Body pattern,
  16 sts and 16 rnds/rows = 4" (10 cm)

INSTRUCTIONS
Boot Cuff (Make 2)

Finished Size:
  5½" long x 14½" upper
  circumference (14 cm x 37 cm)

RIBBING

With Cream, cast on 58 sts, place marker to mark beginning of rnd *(see Circular Knitting and Markers, page 29)*.

Rnds 1-11: (K1, P1) around.

BODY

Rnd 1 (Right side)**:** Knit around.

Rnd 2: Purl around; drop Cream, do **not** cut yarn.

📹 When changing colors, always pick up the new color yarn from **beneath** the dropped yarn and keep the color which has just been worked to the left *(Fig. 2, page 29)*. This will avoid holes in the finished piece. Carry the unused yarn loosely along **wrong** side of piece.

Rnd 3: With Variegated, ★ K1, with yarn in back, slip 1 as if to **purl**; repeat from ★ around.

Rnd 4: ★ P1, with yarn in back, slip 1 as if to **purl**; repeat from ★ around; drop Variegated.

Rnd 5: With Cream, knit around.

Rnd 6: Purl around; drop Cream.

Rnd 7: With Variegated, ★ with yarn in back, slip 1 as if to **purl**, K1; repeat from ★ around.

Rnd 8: ★ With yarn in back, slip 1 as if to **purl**, P1; repeat from ★ around; drop Variegated.

Rnd 9: With Cream, knit around.

Rnd 10: Purl around; drop Cream.

Rnds 11-20: Repeat Rnds 3-10 once, then repeat Rnds 3 and 4 once **more**; at end of Rnd 20, cut Variegated.

Rnd 21: With Cream, knit around.

Rnd 22: Purl around.

Rnds 23 and 24: Repeat Rnds 21 and 22.

Bind off all sts in **knit**.

Ear Warmer

Finished Size: 3½" wide x 18" circumference (9 cm x 45.5 cm)

With Cream, cast on 72 sts, place marker to mark beginning of rnd.

Rnd 1 (Right side)**:** Purl around.

Rnd 2: Knit around.

Rnd 3: Purl around; drop Cream, do **not** cut yarn.

Rnds 4-25: Repeat Boot Cuff Body Rnds 3-10 twice, then repeat Rnds 3-8 once **more**.

Cut Variegated.

Rnd 26: With Cream, knit around.

Rnd 27: Purl around.

Rnds 28 and 29: Repeat Rnds 26 and 27.

Bind off all sts in **purl**.

Scarf

Finished Size: 9¼" wide x 57" long (23.5 cm x 145 cm)

With Cream, cast on 37 sts.

Rows 1 and 2: Knit across; at end of Row 2, drop Cream, do **not** cut yarn.

Carry unused yarn **loosely** along side edge.

Row 3 (Right side)**:** With Variegated, K3, with yarn in back, slip 1 as if to **purl**, ★ K1, with yarn in back, slip 1 as if to **purl**; repeat from ★ across to last 3 sts, K3.

Row 4: K3, with yarn in front, slip 1 as if to **purl**, ★ K1, with yarn in front, slip 1 as if to **purl**; repeat from ★ across to last 3 sts, K3; drop Variegated.

Rows 5 and 6: With Cream, knit across; at end of Row 6, drop Cream.

Row 7: With Variegated, K4, with yarn in back, slip 1 as if to **purl**, ★ K1, with yarn in back, slip 1 as if to **purl**; repeat from ★ across to last 4 sts, K4.

Row 8: K4, with yarn in front, slip 1 as if to **purl**, ★ K1, with yarn in front, slip 1 as if to **purl**; repeat from ★ across to last 4 sts, K4; drop Variegated.

Repeat Rows 1-8 until piece measures approximately 56½" (143.5 cm) from cast on edge, ending by working Row 4 or Row 8; cut Variegated.

Last 3 Rows: Knit across.

Bind off all sts in **knit**.

DOUBLE SEED STITCH SET *continued from page 11.*

Scarf

Finished Size: 9" wide x 57" long (23 cm x 145 cm)

Cast on 36 sts.

Rows 1-8: Slip 1 as if to **knit**, knit across.

Rows 9 and 10: Slip 1 as if to **knit**, K4, P1, (K1, P1) across to last 4 sts, K4.

Rows 11 and 12: Slip 1 as if to **knit**, K3, P1, (K1, P1) across to last 5 sts, K5.

Repeat Rows 9-12 for pattern until piece measures approximately 56" (142 cm) from cast on edge, ending by working Row 9 or Row 11.

Last 8 Rows: Slip 1 as if to **knit**, knit across.

Bind off all sts in **knit**.

GARTER STRIPES SET *continued from page 13.*

Scarf

Finished Size: 9" wide x 57" long (23 cm x 145 cm)

Cast on 36 sts.

Rows 1-12: Slip 1 as if to **knit**, knit across.

Row 13: Slip 1 as if to **knit**, K7, P 20, K8.

Row 14 (Right side)**:** Slip 1 as if to **knit**, knit across.

Rows 15-26: Repeat Rows 13 and 14, 6 times.

Rows 27-32: Slip 1 as if to **knit**, knit across.

Repeat Rows 13-32 for pattern until piece measures approximately 55½" (141 cm) from cast on edge, ending by working Row 25.

Last 12 Rows: Slip 1 as if to **knit**, knit across.

Bind off all sts in **purl**.

HURDLE STITCH SET

 **EASY**

SHOPPING LIST

Yarn (Medium Weight) **4**
[7 ounces, 364 yards
(198 grams, 333 meters) per skein]:
☐ 2 skeins

Knitting Needle
16" (40.5 cm) Circular,
☐ Size 9 (5.5 mm)
or size needed for gauge

Additional Supplies
☐ Marker

GAUGE INFORMATION
In Body pattern,
17 sts and 22 rnds/rows = 4"
(10 cm)

INSTRUCTIONS
Boot Cuff (Make 2)
Finished Size:
6" long x 11¼" upper circumference
(15 cm x 28.5 cm)

RIBBING
Cast on 48 sts, place marker to
mark beginning of rnd *(see Circular
Knitting and Markers, page 29)*.

Rnds 1-11: (K1, P1) around.

BODY
Rnd 1: Knit around.

Rnd 2: Purl around.

Rnds 3 and 4: (K1, P1) around.

Rnds 5-22: Repeat Rnds 1-4, 4 times;
then repeat Rnds 1 and 2 once **more**.

Bind off all sts in **knit**.

Ear Warmer
Finished Size: 4" wide x 17"
circumference (10 cm x 43 cm)

Cast on 72 sts, place marker to mark
beginning of rnd.

Rnd 1: Knit around.

Rnd 2: Purl around.

Rnds 3 and 4: (K1, P1) around.

Rnds 5-22: Repeat Rnds 1-4, 4 times;
then repeat Rnds 1 and 2 once **more**.

Bind off all sts in **purl**.

Scarf

Finished Size: 8" wide x 57" long
   (20.5 cm x 145 cm)

Cast on 34 sts.

Rows 1 and 2: Slip 1 as if to **knit**, knit across.

Rows 3 and 4: Slip 1 as if to **knit**, K2, P1, (K1, P1) 14 times, K2.

Repeat Rows 1-4 for pattern until piece measures approximately 57" (145 cm) from cast on edge, ending by working Row 2.

Bind off all sts in **knit**.

FURRY STRIPES SET

 **EASY**

SHOPPING LIST

Yarn (Medium Weight)
[3.5 ounces, 170 yards
(100 grams, 156 meters) per skein]:
☐ Grey - 3 skeins
(Bulky Weight Novelty)
[1.75 ounces, 64 yards
(50 grams, 58 meters) per skein]:
☐ Red - 3 skeins

Knitting Needle
16" (40.5 cm) Circular,
☐ Size 9 (5.5 mm)
or size needed for gauge

Additional Supplies
☐ Marker

GAUGE INFORMATION
In Body pattern,
16 sts and 30 rnds/rows = 4"
(10 cm)

INSTRUCTIONS
Boot Cuff (Make 2)
Finished Size:
5½" wide x 12" upper
circumference (14 cm x 30.5 cm)

RIBBING
With Grey, cast on 48 sts, place
marker to mark beginning of rnd
*(see Circular Knitting and Markers,
page 29)*.

Rnds 1-11: (K2, P2) around.

BODY
Rnd 1: Knit around.

Rnd 2: Purl around; drop Grey, do **not**
cut yarn.

 When changing colors, always pick
up the new color yarn from **beneath**
the dropped yarn and keep the color
which has just been worked to the
left *(Fig. 2, page 29)*. This will avoid
holes in the finished piece. Carry the
unused yarn loosely along **wrong** side
of piece.

Rnd 3: With Red, knit around.

Rnd 4: Purl around; drop Red.

Rnd 5: With Grey, knit around.

Rnd 6: Purl around; drop Grey.

Rnds 7-22: Repeat Rnds 3-6, 4 times;
at end of Rnd 22, cut Red.

Rnd 23: With Grey, knit around.

Rnd 24: Purl around.

Bind off all sts in **knit**.

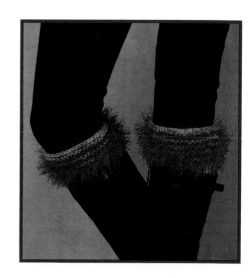

Ear Warmer

Finished Size: 3½" wide x 20"
circumference (9 cm x 51 cm)

With Grey, cast on 80 sts, place marker
to mark beginning of rnd.

Rnd 1: Knit around.

Rnd 2: Purl around.

Rnds 3 and 4: Repeat Rnds 1 and 2; at
end of Rnd 4, drop Grey.

Rnds 5-22: Repeat Boot Cuff Body
Rnds 3-6, 4 times; then repeat Rnds 2
and 3 once **more**.

Cut Red.

Instructions continued on page 27.

TRINITY STITCH SET

▬▬■◻◻ **EASY**

GAUGE INFORMATION

In Body pattern,

    4 repeats (16 sts) and

    22 rnds/rows = 4" (10 cm)

TECHNIQUES USED

📹 (K, P, K) **all** in next st

📹 P3 tog (*Fig. 8, page 31*)

INSTRUCTIONS
Boot Cuff (Make 2)

Finished Size:

    5½" long x 12" upper circumference

    (14 cm x 30.5 cm)

RIBBING

Cast on 48 sts, 📹 place marker to

mark beginning of rnd (*see Circular

Knitting and Markers, page 29*).

Rnds 1-11: (K1, P1) around.

BODY

Rnd 1: ★ (K, P, K) **all** in next st, P3 tog;

repeat from ★ around.

Rnd 2: Knit around.

Rnd 3: ★ P3 tog, (K, P, K) **all** in next st;

repeat from ★ around.

Rnd 4: Knit around.

Rnds 5-18: Repeat Rnds 1-4, 3 times;

then repeat Rnds 1 and 2 once **more**.

Rnd 19: Purl around.

Bind off all sts in **purl**.

Ear Warmer

Finished Size: 4" wide x 18"

    circumference (10 cm x 45.5 cm)

Cast on 72 sts, place marker to mark

beginning of rnd.

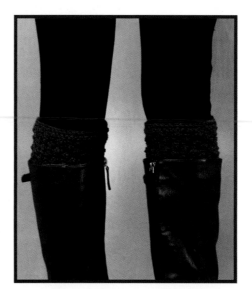

• • • • • •

Rnd 1: Knit around.

Rnd 2: Purl around.

Rnds 3-21: Work same as Boot Cuff Body Rnds 1-19.

Bind off all sts in **purl**.

Scarf

Finished Size: 9" wide x 57" long
   (23 cm x 145 cm)

Cast on 36 sts.

Rows 1-8: Slip 1 as if to **knit**, knit across.

Instructions continued on page 27.

SERPENTINE CABLES SET

EASY

SHOPPING LIST

Yarn (Medium Weight) **4**

[3.5 ounces, 170 yards
(100 grams, 156 meters) per skein]:

☐ 3 skeins

Knitting Needle

16" (40.5 cm) Circular,

☐ Size 8 (5 mm)

or size needed for gauge

Additional Supplies

☐ Marker

☐ Cable needle

STITCH GUIDE

CABLE 4 BACK

(abbreviated C4B) (uses 4 sts)

Slip next 2 sts onto cable needle and hold in **back** of work, K2 from left point, K2 from cable needle.

CABLE 4 FRONT

(abbreviated C4F) (uses 4 sts)

Slip next 2 sts onto cable needle and hold in **front** of work, K2 from left point, K2 from cable needle.

TECHNIQUES USED

Purl increase *(Fig. 4, page 30)*

INSTRUCTIONS
Boot Cuff (Make 2)

Finished Size:

6" long x 11½" upper circumference (15 cm x 29 cm)

RIBBING

Cast on 48 sts, place marker to mark beginning of rnd *(see Circular Knitting and Markers, page 29)*.

Rnds 1-11: (K2, P2) around.

GAUGE INFORMATION

In Body pattern,

3 repeats (21 sts) = 5" (12.75 cm);

20 rnds/rows = 4¼" (10.75 cm)

BODY

Rnd 1: Work purl increase, P1, K4, (P3, K4) around: 49 sts.

Rnds 2-4: (P3, K4) around.

Rnd 5: (P3, C4B) around.

Rnds 6-10: (P3, K4) around.

Rnd 11: (P3, C4F) around.

Rnds 12-16: (P3, K4) around.

Rnd 17: (P3, C4B) around.

Rnds 18-20: (P3, K4) around.

Bind off all sts in **knit**.

Ear Warmer

Finished Size: 4½" wide x 16½" circumference (11.5 cm x 42 cm)

Cast on 70 sts, place marker to mark beginning of rnd.

Rnd 1: Knit around.

Rnd 2: Purl around.

Rnds 3-6: (P3, K4) around.

Rnd 7: (P3, C4B) around.

Rnds 8-12: (P3, K4) around.

Rnd 13: (P3, C4F) around.

Rnds 14-18: (P3, K4) around.

Rnd 19: (P3, C4B) around.

Rnds 20-22: (P3, K4) around.

Rnd 23: Knit around.

Bind off all sts in **knit**.

Scarf

Finished Size: 8¼" wide x 58" long (21 cm x 147.5 cm)

Cast on 40 sts.

Rows 1 and 2: Slip 1 as if to **knit**, knit across.

Row 3: Slip 1 as if to **knit**, K1, P 36, K2.

Row 4: Slip 1 as if to **knit**, K1, P4, (K4, P4) 4 times, K2.

Row 5: Slip 1 as if to **knit**, K5, P4, (K4, P4) 3 times, K6.

Rows 6 and 7: Repeat Rows 4 and 5.

Row 8: Slip 1 as if to **knit**, K1, P4, (C4B, P4) 4 times, K2.

Row 9: Slip 1 as if to **knit**, K5, P4, (K4, P4) 3 times, K6.

Row 10: Slip 1 as if to **knit**, K1, P4, (K4, P4) 4 times, K2.

Rows 11-13: Repeat Rows 9 and 10 once, then repeat Row 9 once **more**.

Row 14: Slip 1 as if to **knit**, K1, P4, (C4F, P4) 4 times, K2.

Row 15: Slip 1 as if to **knit**, K5, P4, (K4, P4) 3 times, K6.

Repeat Rows 4-15 for pattern until piece measures approximately 57¾" (147 cm) from cast on edge, ending by working Row 5.

Last 2 Rows: Slip 1 as if to **knit**, knit across.

Bind off all sts in **knit**.

FURRY STRIPES SET *continued from page 21.*

Rnd 23: With Grey, knit around.

Rnd 24: Purl around.

Rnds 25 and 26: Repeat Rnds 23 and 24.
Bind off all sts in **knit**.

Scarf

Finished Size: 8" wide x 57" long (20.5 cm x 145 cm)

With Grey, cast on 32 sts.

Rows 1-7: Knit across; at end of Row 7, drop Grey.

Carry unused yarn **loosely** along side edge; do **not** cut yarn until instructed.

Rows 8 and 9: With Red, knit across; at end of Row 9, drop Red.

Rows 10 and 11: With Grey, knit across; at end of Row 11, drop Grey.

Rows 12-25: Repeat Rows 8-11, 3 times; then repeat Rows 8 and 9 once **more**; at end of Row 25, cut Red.

Rows 26-43: With Grey, knit across.

Repeat Rows 8-43 for pattern until piece measures approximately 56" (142 cm) from cast on edge, ending by working Row 25.

Last 8 Rows: With Grey, slip 1 as if to **knit**, knit across.

Bind off all sts in **knit**.

TRINITY STITCH SET *continued from page 23.*

Row 9: Slip 1 as if to **knit**, K3, ★ (K, P, K) all in next st, P3 tog; repeat from ★ 6 times **more**, K4.

Row 10: Slip 1 as if to **knit**, K3, P 28, K4.

Row 11: Slip 1 as if to **knit**, K3, ★ P3 tog, (K, P, K) all in next st; repeat from ★ 6 times **more**, K4.

Row 12: Slip 1 as if to **knit**, K3, P 28, K4.

Repeat Rows 9-12 for pattern until piece measures approximately 56" (142 cm) from cast on edge, ending by working Row 12.

Last 6 Rows: Slip 1 as if to **knit**, knit across.

Bind off all sts in **knit**.

GENERAL INSTRUCTIONS

ABBREVIATIONS

C4B	Cable 4 Back
C4F	Cable 4 Front
cm	centimeters
K	knit
mm	millimeters
P	purl
Rnd(s)	Round(s)
st(s)	stitch(es)
tog	together
YO	yarn over

KNIT TERMINOLOGY	
UNITED STATES	**INTERNATIONAL**
gauge =	tension
bind off =	cast off
yarn over (YO) =	yarn forward (yfwd) **or** yarn around needle (yrn)

SYMBOLS & TERMS

★ — work instructions following ★ as many **more** times as indicated in addition to the first time.

( ) or [ ] — work enclosed instructions as **many** times as specified by the number immediately following **or** work all enclosed instructions in the stitch indicated **or** contains explanatory remarks.

colon (:) — the number(s) given after a colon at the end of a row or round denote(s) the number of stitches you should have on that row or round.

GAUGE

Exact gauge is **essential** for proper size. Before beginning your project, make a sample swatch in the yarn and needle specified. After completing the swatch, measure it, counting your stitches and rows or rounds carefully. If your swatch is larger or smaller than specified, **make another, changing needle size to get the correct gauge.** Keep trying until you find the size needle that will give you the specified gauge.

Yarn Weight Symbol & Names	LACE 0	SUPER FINE 1	FINE 2	LIGHT 3	MEDIUM 4	BULKY 5	SUPER BULKY 6	JUMBO 7
Type of Yarns in Category	Fingering, size 10 crochet thread	Sock, Fingering, Baby	Sport, Baby	DK, Light Worsted	Worsted, Afghan, Aran	Chunky, Craft, Rug	Super Bulky, Roving	Jumbo, Roving
Knit Gauge Ranges in Stockinette St to 4" (10 cm)	33-40 sts**	27-32 sts	23-26 sts	21-24 sts	16-20 sts	12-15 sts	7-11 sts	6 sts and fewer
Advised Needle Size Range	000 to 1	1 to 3	3 to 5	5 to 7	7 to 9	9 to 11	11 to 17	17 and larger

* GUIDELINES ONLY: The chart above reflects the most commonly used gauges and needle sizes for specific yarn categories.

** Lace weight yarns are usually knitted on larger needles to create lacy openwork patterns. Accordingly, a gauge range is difficult to determine. Always follow the gauge stated in your pattern.

■□□□ BEGINNER	Projects for first-time knitters using basic knit and purl stitches. Minimal shaping.
■■□□ EASY	Projects using basic stitches, repetitive stitch patterns, simple color changes, and simple shaping and finishing.
■■■□ INTERMEDIATE	Projects with a variety of stitches, such as basic cables and lace, simple intarsia, double-pointed needles and knitting in the round needle techniques, mid-level shaping and finishing.
■■■■ EXPERIENCED	Projects using advanced techniques and stitches, such as short rows, fair isle, more intricate intarsia, cables, lace patterns, and numerous color changes.

CIRCULAR KNITTING

Cast on all stitches as instructed. Untwist and straighten the stitches on the needle to be sure that the cast on ridge lays on the inside of the needle and never rolls around the needle.

Hold the needle so that the ball of yarn is attached to the stitch closest to the right hand point. Place a marker on the right hand point to mark the beginning of the round. Working each round on the outside of the the circle with the **right** side of the knitting facing you, work across the stitches on the left hand point *(Fig. 1)*.

Check to be sure that the cast on edge has not twisted around the needle. If it has, it is impossible to untwist it. The only way to fix this is to rip it out and return to the cast on row.

MARKERS

As a convenience to you, we have used markers to help distinguish the beginning of a round. Place markers as instructed. You may use purchased markers or tie a length of contrasting color yarn around the needle. When you reach a marker on each round, slip it from the left needle point to the right needle point; remove it when no longer needed.

CHANGING COLORS

When changing colors, always pick up the new color yarn from **beneath** the dropped yarn and keep the color which has just been worked to the left *(Fig. 2)*.

Fig. 2

Fig. 1

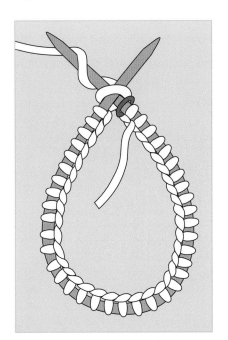

KNITTING NEEDLES																			
U.S.	0	1	2	3	4	5	6	7	8	9	10	10½	11	13	15	17	19	35	50
U.K.	13	12	11	10	9	8	7	6	5	4	3	2	1	00	000	---	---	---	---
Metric - mm	2	2.25	2.75	3.25	3.5	3.75	4	4.5	5	5.5	6	6.5	8	9	10	12.75	15	19	25

INCREASES

KNIT INCREASE

Knit the next stitch but do **not** slip the old stitch off the left needle *(Fig. 3a)*. Insert the right needle into the **back** loop of the **same** stitch and knit it *(Fig. 3b)*, then slip the old stitch off the left needle.

Fig. 3a

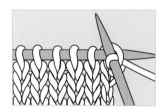

Fig. 3b

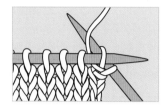

PURL INCREASE

Purl the next stitch but do **not** slip the old stitch off the left needle. Insert the right needle into the **back** loop of the same stitch from **back** to **front** *(Fig. 4)* and purl it. Slip the old stitch off the left needle.

Fig. 4

YARN OVERS *(abbreviated YO)*

After a knit stitch, before a purl stitch

Bring the yarn forward **between** the needles, then back **over** the top of the right hand needle and forward **between** the needles again, so that it is now in position to purl the next stitch *(Fig. 5a)*.

Fig. 5a

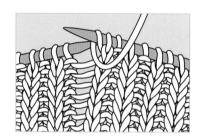

After a purl stitch, before a knit stitch

Take the yarn **over** the right hand needle to the back, so that it is now in position to knit the next stitch *(Fig. 5b)*.

Fig. 5b

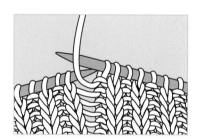

DECREASES

KNIT 2 TOGETHER *(abbreviated K2 tog)*

Insert the right needle into the **front** of the first two stitches on the left needle as if to **knit** *(Fig. 6)*, then **knit** them together as if they were one stitch.

Fig. 6

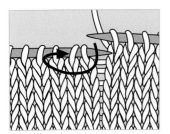

PURL 3 TOGETHER *(abbreviated P3 tog)*

Insert the right needle into the **front** of the first three stitches on the left needle as if to **purl** *(Fig. 8)*, then **purl** them together as if they were one stitch.

Fig. 8

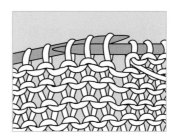

PURL 2 TOGETHER *(abbreviated P2 tog)*

Insert the right needle into the **front** of the first two stitches on the left needle as if to **purl** *(Fig. 7)*, then **purl** them together as if they were one stitch.

Fig. 7

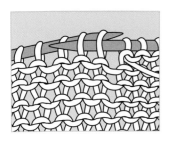

YARN INFORMATION

The projects in this book were made using Medium Weight Yarn with Furry Stripes Set also using a Bulky Weight Yarn. Any brand of the specified weight of yarn may be used. It is best to refer to the yardage/meters when determining how many balls or skeins to purchase. Remember, to arrive at the finished size, it is the GAUGE/TENSION that is important, not the brand of yarn. For your convenience, listed below are the specific yarns used to create our photography models. Because yarn manufacturers make frequent changes in their product lines, you may sometimes find it necessary to use a substitute yarn or to search for the discontinued product at alternate suppliers (locally or online).

CHEVRON SEED STITCH SET

Lion Brand® Vanna's Choice®

#180 Cranberry

LITTLE SHELLS SET

Red Heart® Super Saver®

#336 Warm Brown

ARCHING CABLES SET

Lion Brand® Vanna's Choice®

#175 Radiant Lime

DOUBLE SEED STITCH SET

Lion Brand® Vanna's Choice®

#102 Aqua

GARTER STRIPES SET

Red Heart® Super Saver®

#321 Gold

SLIP STITCH SET

Lion Brand® Vanna's Choice®
Baby

Cream - #098 Lamb

Lion Brand® Vanna's Choice®

Variegated - #500 Patchwork Grey

HURDLE STITCH SET

Red Heart® Super Saver®

#3862 Jade

FURRY STRIPES SET

Lion Brand® Vanna's Choice®

Grey - #149 Silver Grey

Lion Brand® Fun Fur®

Red - #113 Red

TRINITY STITCH SET

Lion Brand® Vanna's Choice®

#145 Eggplant

SERPENTINE CABLES SET

Lion Brand® Vanna's Choice®

#099 Linen

We have made every effort to ensure that these instructions are accurate and complete. We cannot, however, be responsible for human error, typographical mistakes, or variations in individual work.

Production Team: Writer/Instructional Editor - Sarah J. Green; Editorial Writer - Susan Frantz Wiles; Senior Graphic Artist - Lora Puls; Graphic Artist - Victoria Temple; Photo Stylist - Lori Wenger; and Photographer - Jason Masters.